MAKERS
As Innovators

Sphero

CHERRY LAKE PUBLISHING • ANN ARBOR, MICHIGAN

by Adrienne Matteson

CHERRY LAKE
Publishing

A Note to Adults: Please review the instructions for the activities in this book before allowing children to do them. Be sure to help them with any activities you do not think they can safely complete on their own.

A Note to Kids: Be sure to ask an adult for help with these activities when you need it. Always put your safety first!

Published in the United States of America by Cherry Lake Publishing
Ann Arbor, Michigan
www.cherrylakepublishing.com

Series Adviser: Kristin Fontichiaro
Photo Credits: All images by Adrienne Matteson

Library of Congress Cataloging-in-Publication Data
Names: Matteson, Adrienne, author.
Title: Sphero / by Adrienne Matteson.
Other titles: 21st century skills innovation library. Makers as innovators.
Description: Ann Arbor, Michigan : Cherry Lake Publishing, [2017] | Series: 21st Century Skills Innovation Library.
    Makers as innovators | Audience: Grades 4 to 6. | Includes bibliographical references and index.
Identifiers: LCCN 2016055214| ISBN 9781634726856 [lib. bdg.] | ISBN 9781634727181 [pbk.] |
    ISBN 9781634727518 [pdf] | ISBN 9781634727846 [ebook]
Subjects: LCSH: Robots–Programming–Juvenile literature. |
    Robots–Control   systems–Juvenile literature.
Classification: LCC TJ211.2 .M3745 2017 | DDC 629.8/92–dc23LC record available
    at https://lccn.loc.gov/2016055214

Cherry Lake Publishing would like to acknowledge the work of the Partnership for
21st Century Learning. Please visit www.p21.org for more information.

Printed in the United States of America
Corporate Graphics

Contents

Chapter 1

Have a Ball!

Would you like to meet one of the most incredible robots available today? On its own, it doesn't look like much more than a plastic ball. But when you connect it to a smartphone or tablet, it comes alive with light and movement. This little ball is capable of sensing and responding to its own **acceleration** and direction. It can react to collisions and falling. It even knows the temperature.

Sphero is easy to program and control using a tablet computer.

It is complex enough to challenge master programmers and simple enough to be a tool for elementary school students. Meet Sphero, the "little ball that does it all."

Sphero is an app-controlled robotic ball. It uses wireless Bluetooth signals to connect to apps on tablets and smartphones, and becomes a working part of the app. There are dozens of Sphero apps. Within them, Sphero takes on many different roles. Sphero can be driven around like a remote-controlled car, used as the joystick for a game you are playing, follow a path you draw on your tablet, or react to being grabbed as part of a multiplayer game. At its most sophisticated, Sphero can run a complex program you have coded yourself. Sphero's abilities will grow along with your programming skills and your imagination.

How It All Began

Sphero was invented in 2010 and launched in 2011 by **engineers** Adam Wilson and Ian Bernstein. The two men wanted to use their smartphones to control objects in the real world. At first, they used their phones like remote controls to turn on lights

The Sphero Family

Orbotix makes five different Sphero robots. Be sure to choose the one that suits you best.

- **Sphero:** This is the basic Sphero robot. The current model is Sphero 2.0. Sphero is programmable. It also works with most Sphero apps that are available for iOS, Android, Chrome, and Kindle.
- **SPRK and SPRK+:** The SPRK and SPRK+ model Spheros are designed for school use. They give students the chance to write computer programs and put them into action. SPRK models have clear shells so you can see how everything inside works.
- **BB-8:** This is a special Sphero designed to look and behave like the droid from the film *Star Wars: The Force Awakens*. BB-8 Sphero can respond to voices and has a strong personality.
- **Force Band:** This is a *Star Wars*-themed wristband that allows the wearer to control connected robots with hand gestures.
- **Ollie:** This robot is made for racing. Ollie is shaped like a tube with a tire on each end. It can move at speeds up to 14 miles (22.5 kilometers) per hour!

and start cars. But they wanted to take on a bigger challenge and use the technology for something more fun. Bernstein was a big fan of robotics. He had been inventing robots since he was in middle school. Wilson also liked to tinker and make stuff, so inventing a robot was the perfect project.

Wilson and Bernstein attended a Techstars event in 2010. Techstars is a company made up of investors who give promising new companies the funding and guidance they need to make their ideas a reality. The two engineers made a big impression. Techstars gave them everything they needed to get the ball rolling. Sphero was introduced to the world in 2011.

A student uses tablet controls to get Sphero rolling.

Chapter 2

How Sphero Works

While it may look like a simple ball, Sphero is actually a product of advanced engineering and **software** programming. In order for Sphero to roll easily in all directions, it needs to follow very specific directions, such as "Move forward at 20 degrees left and 50 percent speed for 3

There's a lot more to Sphero than meets the eye.

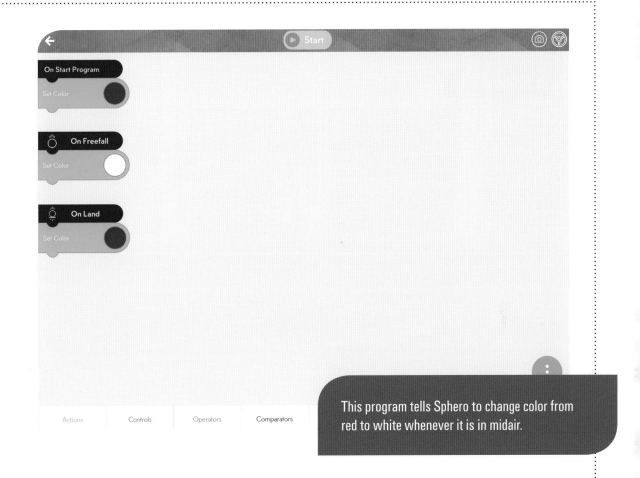

This program tells Sphero to change color from red to white whenever it is in midair.

seconds and then stop." A robot that can follow those directions needs to be able to sense the world around it. Sphero is unique because it understands what direction it is facing, if it is moving in any direction, how quickly it is moving, and if it is moving up or down. It can remember its directions even after colliding with another object. It's a pretty smart little ball.

Understanding how to use Sphero requires knowing about the many parts that make the robot work.

The First Sphero

The first Sphero **prototype** that Ian Bernstein and Adam Wilson brought with them to Techstars in 2010 was much different from the Sphero we have today. At the time, the device wasn't called Sphero. It was called Gearbox. The robotic ball had an all-black shell and no **LED** lights, and it worked with an app called Sumo. The ball could be controlled by tilting the smartphone from side to side and front to back.

The two men wanted to make their robot faster, create more apps, and make it more fun to use. Sphero was only ready to launch after a year of creating prototype after prototype, visiting **maker** gatherings, and holding "hack weekends" for programmers to work on Sphero apps. When one of your own projects is taking a long time to perfect, remember how long it took Bernstein and Wilson to get Sphero just right. Don't give up!

Circuit Board

Inside every Sphero is a circuit board that houses the programmable part of the robot. It includes a few key parts:

- **Accelerometer:** This measures the changes in Sphero's speed.
- **Gyroscope:** This helps balance the robot inside Sphero on its two wheels. The gyroscope

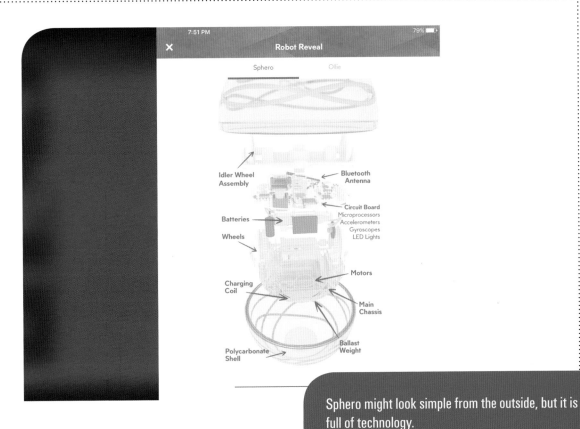

Sphero might look simple from the outside, but it is full of technology.

is also what allows the robot to know where its front and back are and to change directions.

- **Bluetooth antenna:** This allows the robot to communicate wirelessly with your smartphone or tablet.
- **LED lights:** The circuit board holds two LED lights that can be programmed to change colors, as well as the tiny taillight that shows you which side of the robot is its back.

Inductive charging coil: The batteries inside Sphero are charged using inductive charging. This is a way to transfer energy using an electromagnetic field instead of cables. That field is created by copper coils inside both Sphero and its charging base. Because there aren't any holes in Sphero to plug in cables, the robot can be completely sealed and waterproof!

Motors: Sphero has two motors. Each one is connected to a wheel. The motors can be programmed to work together or separately. You should see what happens when the motors are turning at different speeds!

Ballast weight: This weighs down the robot to provide the wheels with enough **friction** to grip the robot's plastic shell and make it move as they spin.

Chapter 3

Programming Sphero

The **language** used to write programs for Sphero is called Oval. You do not need to know Oval to play with your Sphero. There are many apps that will allow you to just connect and play. But if you want to give your Sphero commands of your own, you will need to use Oval. Luckily, there is a version of

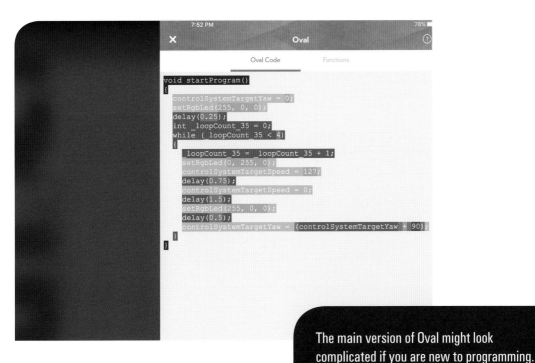

The main version of Oval might look complicated if you are new to programming.

Oval Code

The Oval programming language is unique to Sphero. However, it is similar to other programming languages. At any time, you can change your view in Lightning Lab so you can see your program in Oval code instead of blocks. Just tap on the three dots and select "Oval Code (</>)". This is great to do if you are curious about learning more advanced programming skills.

Oval that is easy to understand even for beginning programmers.

The app used to write programs in Oval code is called SPRK Lightning Lab. Lightning Lab was created to work with the SPRK models of Sphero. It can also be used for Sphero 2.0 and Ollie. It contains several example programs that you can copy and change however you like. This is a great way to get to know the code and your robot.

Code Blocks

The blocks you will use the most when you first get started writing code are the Actions, Controls, and Events blocks.

- **Actions:** These are the blocks that command Sphero to do things such as "Roll," "Stop," or "Set Color."

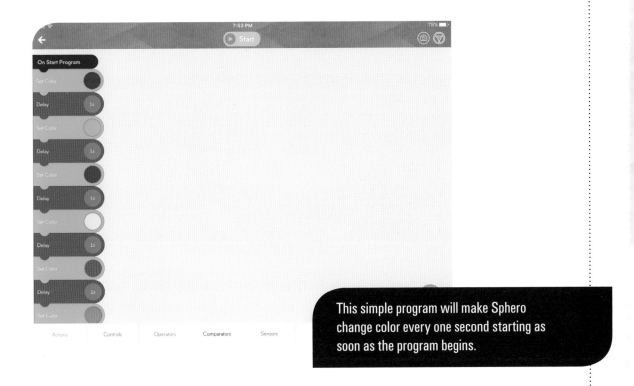

This simple program will make Sphero change color every one second starting as soon as the program begins.

- **Controls:** These blocks control how an action happens. For example, a "Loop" control will cause the action to happen over and over. The "If/Then" control block sets an action to happen only in certain situations.
- **Events:** These blocks control when a program will begin. Will it begin when you tap "Start"? Or when Sphero collides with something?

Blocks of code work together to create more complex programs. A complex program can respond

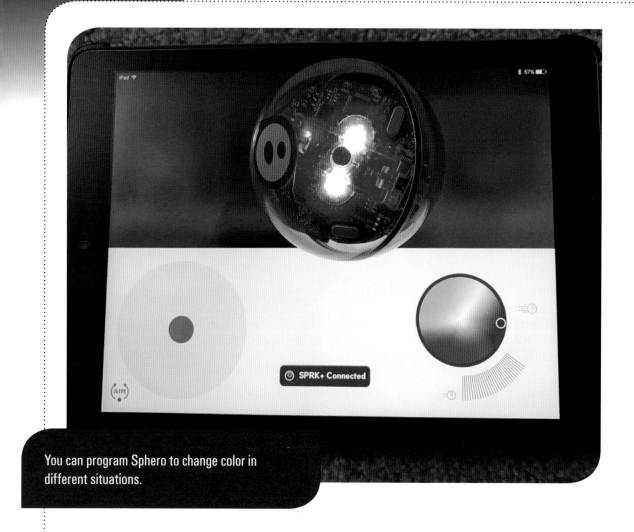

You can program Sphero to change color in different situations.

differently to various situations. For example, you might program your Sphero to change colors when it is accelerating or falling. Or you might program it to change directions when it collides with another object. To accomplish these tasks, you will need to use more advanced code blocks.

- **Functions:** In programming, a function is a set of instructions the program will follow in exactly the same way every time it is triggered. In Oval, function blocks allow you to create and name new functions to be used in your program.

- **Variables:** In programming, a variable is something that can change depending on what is happening. It is also a way to store information inside a program. In Oval, variable blocks allow you to create and name new variables.
- **Operators and comparators:** These blocks are mathematical commands. Operators are "Add," "Subtract," "Multiply," and "Divide." Comparators include "Equal," "Greater Than," and "Not Equal." Together they can be used within a function to define how a variable will be used.
- **Sensors:** These blocks tell Sphero what information it needs to collect to run the program. Does it need to know if it is speeding up? Use the "Accelerometer" sensor. Does it need to know what direction it is facing? Use the "Orientation" sensor.

A guide created by SPRK Education lists every block and how to use it. Find it at: *https://sprk.docsapp.io/.*

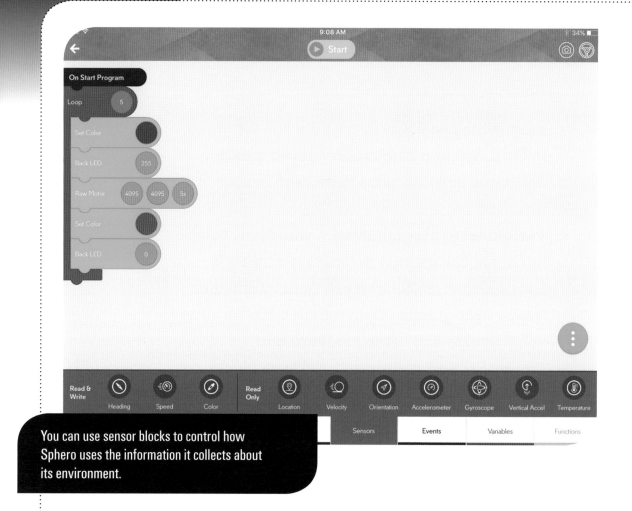

You can use sensor blocks to control how Sphero uses the information it collects about its environment.

Remixing

The best way to get started on any new programming language is to remix, or change, an existing sample program. The SPRK Lightning Lab comes with about a dozen sample programs for you to copy and remix. This will give you a chance to see how different parts of code work and what happens when you make changes to variables.

Give It a Try

Open up the SPRK Lightning Lab app on your device
and connect your Sphero using Bluetooth. Locate the
"Lights" sample program and open the editing window.
Run the program once to see how it works. Then try
changing one block at a time to create something new.
Note how the action and control blocks work together.

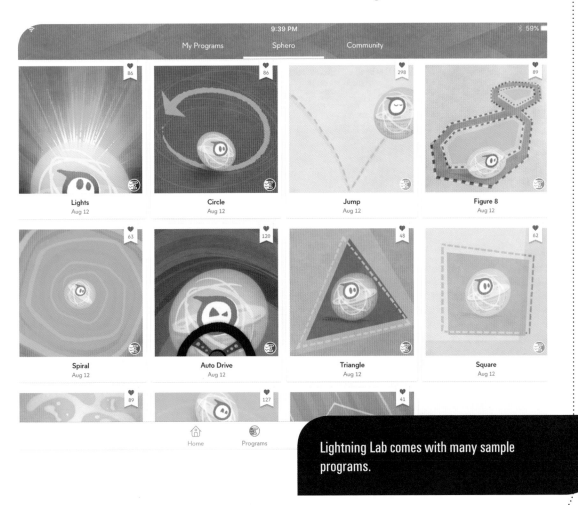

Lightning Lab comes with many sample programs.

Chapter 4

Putting It All Together

Once you have remixed a few sample programs, you will be ready to use your programming skills to solve more complex problems. One great way to test your coding (and driving) skills is to create a maze and program Sphero to navigate through it.

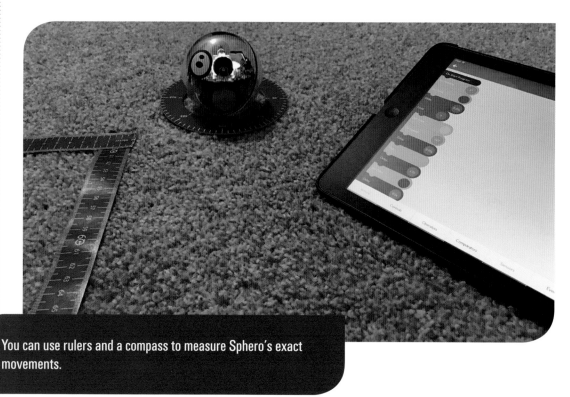

You can use rulers and a compass to measure Sphero's exact movements.

MacroLab

There is another way to write programs for Sphero. The MacroLab app for Sphero 2.0 and Ollie predates Oval and the Lightning Lab. In MacroLab, you can use a programming language made of easy-to-understand symbols to create mini programs called macros. Like Lightning Lab, MacroLab comes with several example macros you can use to learn how it works. Because it is simpler, MacroLab can help you understand the more complex language of Oval.

You will need:
- Sphero and a tablet or smartphone
- Masking tape for marking the edges of the maze
- A protractor for measuring angles (If you have a SPRK or SPRK+ Sphero, a protractor came in the box.)
- A tape measure or a yardstick
- A stopwatch

Begin by building your maze. Use as much space as you wish, but try to keep your lines straight. You can keep the whole maze in one space or make a path through your home or school. Be sure to ask for permission to use the space before you start.

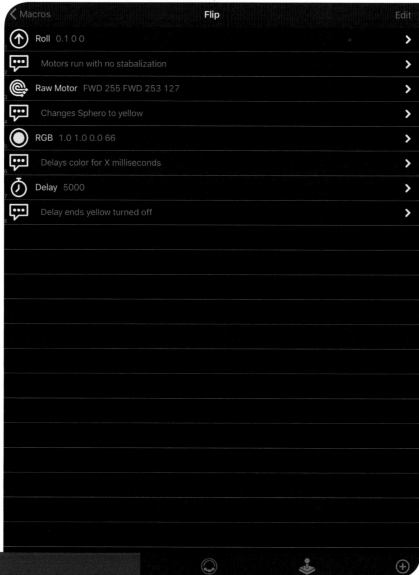

Try using MacroLab to program Sphero.

When you have your maze laid out, test it out by driving your Sphero through it. Once you are happy with it, measure the length of each segment and note the distances on paper. You may choose to sketch a model of your maze on paper so you can keep track of distances more easily.

Create a new program in Lightning Lab. Place blocks to program Sphero's path through the maze one segment at a time. Sphero cannot tell distance, but it can travel for a set number of seconds and at a set speed. This means you will need to test how long it takes your Sphero to travel each segment of the maze

Make sure Sphero stays inside the lines as it travels through your maze.

at your chosen speed. You will also need to set the heading, or direction, for Sphero's path. For the heading, use your protractor to measure each angle that Sphero needs to turn in order to follow the path.

Use the "Roll" and "Stop" blocks to navigate Sphero down each segment of the maze. Use the "Set Heading" or "Spin" blocks to make Sphero turn for the next segment. Try using the "Delay" block if you want Sphero to pause between segments. If you want, use the "Set Color" block to change Sphero's colors with each turn. Run your program after you code each segment of the maze.

If you are having trouble finding the right combination of code blocks to navigate through the maze, take a look at the example programs again. The "Triangle" and "Square" programs have all the tools you will need in them.

Once you have successfully programmed Sphero to make it through the maze, set a new challenge. Can you make Sphero go faster? Spin twice at every corner? Flash red every time it turns? The choice is yours, and the possibilities are endless.

Chapter 5

Spark Your Imagination

n 2014, the Sphero company launched SPRK Education. SPRK is pronounced "spark." It stands for "schools parents robots kids." The SPRK program includes the SPRK and SPRK+ Sphero models, which have clear shells and are packaged with maker tools such as protractors and measuring tape.

The clear shell of the SPRK+ Sphero lets you see clearly what is inside your robot.

SPRK is also a community of educators and learners. The hub of that community is the Lightning Lab app. Lightning Lab allows users to access a news feed full of ideas and projects that other Sphero users have posted. In Lightning Lab, you can try out lessons and challenges that have been posted by the Sphero team, other users, or even your teachers. It also has several lessons titled "Blocks." These teach new users the ins and outs of creating programs for Sphero.

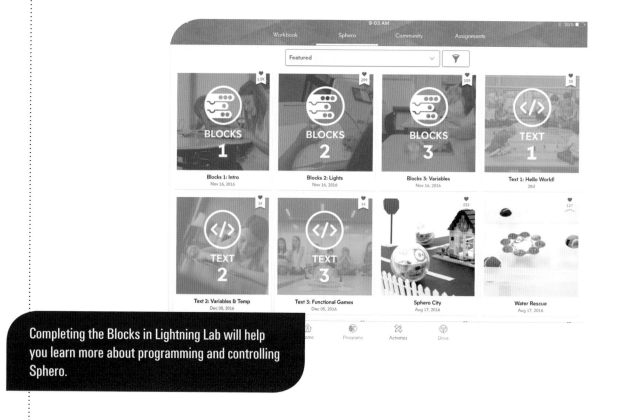

Completing the Blocks in Lightning Lab will help you learn more about programming and controlling Sphero.

The programs you create in Lightning Lab can be shared online with the Sphero community. Sharing is a big part of being a maker. The programs you create and share can be borrowed and remixed by other Sphero users. Who knows? Maybe a program you write will help solve a big problem for Sphero users around the world!

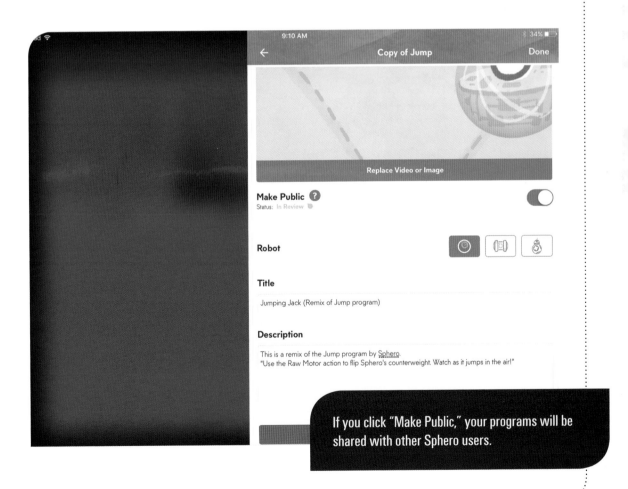

If you click "Make Public," your programs will be shared with other Sphero users.

Making with Sphero

With its simple round shape, bright lights, durable outside, and powerful inside, Sphero is a fantastic maker tool. Many of the activities in Lightning Lab show you how you can use Sphero as a piece of larger inventions. Don't forget, Sphero is waterproof, and it can swim!

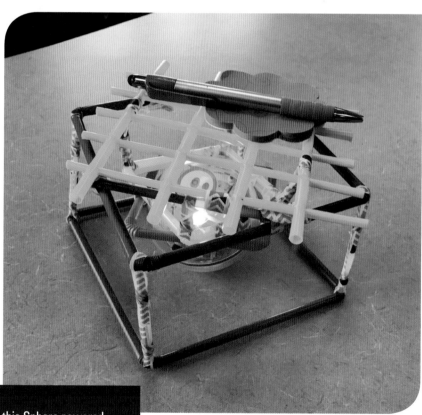

Place items on top of this Sphero-powered vehicle and let Sphero drive them around.

Painting with Sphero

Sphero is waterproof. This means it is paint-proof, too! Get creative with Sphero and use it to make art. Try driving your Sphero through washable paints on butcher paper. Or program Sphero to write words or draw a picture.

Covering Sphero up before painting will add texture and make it easier to clean up afterward. Try putting it inside a small plastic bag or wrapping it in plastic wrap. Then paint away!

Take a Sphero maker challenge! Try making one of the following:

- A Sphero-powered car that can carry snacks to your friends.
- A Ferris wheel or merry-go-round powered by Sphero.
- A Sphero-powered boat that can stay afloat and win a race.

Glossary

acceleration (ak-sel-uh-RAY-shun) in increase in speed

engineers (en-juh-NEERZ) people who are trained to design and build things

friction (FRIK-shun) the force that slows down objects as they rub against each other

language (LANG-wij) a set of words, symbols, and rules that work together to create a computer program; there are many programming languages

LED (EL EE DEE) a small light that uses very little energy and gives off very little heat; LED stands for "light-emitting diode"

maker (MAY-kur) a creative person who makes everything from artwork and useful objects to robots and computer programs

prototype (PROH-tuh-tipe) the first version of an invention that tests an idea to see if it will work

software (SAWFT-wair) computer programs that control the workings of the equipment, or hardware, and direct it to do specific tasks

Find Out More

BOOKS

Benson, Pete. *Scratch*. Ann Arbor, MI: Cherry Lake Publishing, 2016.

Gilby, Nancy Benovich. *FIRST Robotics*. Ann Arbor, MI: Cherry Lake Publishing, 2016.

Roslund, Samantha, and Kristin Fontichiaro. *Maker Faire*. Ann Arbor, MI: Cherry Lake Publishing, 2014.

WEB SITES

Lightning Lab
http://edu.sphero.com
Get started with the Sphero Lightning Lab.

Oval Language for Sphero Robots
https://sprk.docsapp.io/docs/get-started
Learn everything there is to know about Oval programming.

Sphero Blog
http://blog.sphero.com
Find out what Sphero's creators are up to and how people are using Sphero in interesting ways.

Index

About the Author

Adrienne Matteson is a school librarian. She spends most of her days playing with robots and helping her students write programs about unicorns.